# Suffolk
# Shipping

Barges in the entrance lock waiting to enter Ipswich Dock, *c*.1900.

# Suffolk Shipping

## Mike Stammers

TEMPUS

Scottish fishing boats leaving Lowestoft, *c*.1914.

First published 2003

Tempus Publishing Limited
The Mill, Brimscombe Port,
Stroud, Gloucestershire, GL5 2QG

© Mike Stammers, 2003

The right of Mike Stammers to be identified as the Author
of this work has been asserted in accordance with the
Copyrights, Designs and Patents Act 1988.

British Library Cataloguing in Publication Data.
A catalogue record for this book is available from the British Library.

ISBN 0 7524 2812 8

Typesetting and origination by Tempus Publishing Limited
Printed in Great Britain by Midway Colour Print, Wiltshire

# Contents

# Acknowledgements

I am grateful to the following people and organisations for the accompanying pictures and in particular to Bob Malster for his generosity in lending me so many pictures from his collection:
Bob Malster: frontispiece, p.25, p.30 top, p.28-29, p.33 bottom, p.44, p.46, p.47, p.53 top and bottom, p.55, p.56-57, p.58 bottom, p.60 bottom, p.61 bottom, p.62 top, p.63 top, p.64 bottom, p.66 top, p.80 top and bottom, p.85 to p.89 all, p.93 bottom, p.94 top, p.102, p.107, p.109, p.114 and 115 top and bottom, p.118 top, p.120 to 127 top and bottom, p.128 top; also nos 68, 83.
The Moot Hall Aldeburgh: p.104 top and p.111 bottom;
Bergen Maritime Museum: p.50 bottom;
British Transport Docks (now ABP) p.72 top;
Chamber of Shipping: p.70 bottom;
David Clement: p.51 top and bottom, p.52 bottom;
Valerie Fenwick: p.11 bottom, p.12 top and bottom, p.13 bottom;
Campbell McCutcheon: p.82 top, p.112 bottom, p.118 bottom, p.119 top and bottom;
Trustees of National Museums, Liverpool: p.23 bottom, p.66 bottom, p.67 top, p.91 top, p.120 bottom;
Norfolk Museums Service – Great Yarmouth Museums and their Maritime Curator, James Steward: p.9 bottom, p.49 top, p.90 top;
Omell Galleries, London: p.24 top;
Adrian Osler: p.17;
Suffolk Record Office: p.54 top and bottom. Nos 59, 65, 66.

Oulton Broad, with the excursion steamer *Gorleston* in Mutford Lock, c.1950.

# Introduction

This is a pictorial history of the ships and boats that have been built, owned, and sailed to and from the county of Suffolk. It is based on a wide selection of images in different media, ranging from photographs to paintings, drawings, models and archaeological remains. The choice is simply my own. I confess that I have always been very enthusiastic about Thames barges and they have a section to themselves as a result. These marvellously versatile craft traded in large numbers to Suffolk ports and it was still possible to see them carrying commercial cargoes to the Ipswich flour mills into the early 1960s. As such they were one of the last fleets of commercial sailing vessels in Europe and it was a privilege to be able to watch and photograph them.

There have been a number of picture histories on the ports of Suffolk and I have tried to avoid covering the same ground, and so the emphasis is on the ships rather than the development of the ports and their facilities. I have also tried to look for unused or different images and where necessary I have 'imported' a picture of a ship from elsewhere if it is a useful in depicting a particular kind of Suffolk vessel.

Suffolk is almost surrounded by water: to the north there are the Rivers Waveney and Little Ouse which form the boundary with Norfolk; to the west the River Lark; to the south the River Stour forms the boundary with Essex; to the east there is the North Sea. The latter was and is a water highway to the Thames and London. In the heyday of the North East coal trade, hundreds of sailing colliers' vessels negotiated the complex of shoals off the Suffolk coast and the lighthouses at Lowestoft and Orford were welcome beacons on their passage. Many ran aground and were lost, especially in the winter gales. Help was at hand from the rowing and sailing lifeboats based in most of the coastal settlements or from the salvage companies based between Lowestoft and Southwold that employed fast beach yawls. Today, the coastal trade is much reduced. The coal trade has gone and has been replaced by the traffic in fuel, oil, petrol and diesel from the refineries to local distribution depots. On the other hand, other bulk cargoes such as grain, stone and timber are still carried by coaster. There are also new trades such as the delivery of steel plate usually from abroad and coastal container services. There are also many fewer coasters, for not only has trade declined but the size of ship has increased substantially. If you look at F.T. Everard's fleet – one of the most commonly seen on the Suffolk coast and in Suffolk ports – their ship *Sociality* of 1953 could carry about 800 tons while the *Sociality* of 1986 could lift 2,400 tons.

Suffolk's maritime past certainly goes back before the Roman occupation of Britain in the first century AD. But it was they who left the first substantial remains which imply maritime activity. The surviving walls of their fortress of Burgh Castle on Breydon Water are tangible evidence of their huge naval effort to protect the coast from Anglo-Saxon raiders. That effort proved abortive as the whole infrastructure of the western Roman Empire collapsed in the fifth century. This left the East Coast open not only to raids but also to peaceful settlement: a number of Anglo-Saxon kingdoms including the pagan rulers of Suffolk. One of their kings, probably Raedwald (*c*.596-625), was buried at Sutton Hoo in a large clinker-built ship with a magnificent collection of grave goods.

The trade that the Anglo-Saxon kingdoms had built up with the Continent continued to expand in the later Middle Ages after the Norman Conquest of 1066. For Suffolk, this meant commodities like wool, woollen cloth and pickled herring. Major ports included Ipswich, and Dunwich. The importance of maritime trade can be clearly seen in the official seals of these boroughs which all carry images of ships. Up to the fourteenth century Dunwich was probably the most important. It was a large town with fifty-two churches. In Edward I's reign the town's people owned eleven warships, sixteen 'fair ships' (presumably large vessels), twenty barks and twenty-four fishing boats. But the sea's encroachment inexorably washed most of the town away and Dunwich today is no more than a hamlet. This constant erosion and re-deposition of the seashore sands and gravel has been a continuing factor for the county's seafarers. For example, the mouth of the River Ore leading to Orford and Aldeburgh has gradually moved south and the gravel bar is still shifting; one year the main channel will lie close to the shore and by the next a new entrance has been formed off to the seaward side through the outer bank of shingle.

The river estuaries were also a vital part in the development of local shipping. Before railways and efficient road transport they were the most efficient way of transporting goods and passengers. Ipswich and Woodbridge were strategically sited at the head of tidal estuaries. Carriage by water was extended up the inland rivers by dredging them and building locks.

The Waveney was canalised to Bungay in 1670; the Stour was opened for twenty-five miles for trade to Sudbury in 1705; the Blyth to Halesworth in 1761; the Gipping to Stowmarket in 1793. We should also add the River Lark: a tributary of the Great Ouse which was canalised to Bury St Edmunds, the main town in the west of the county. The link with the great Ouse made it possible for the town to receive coal by water from the port of King's Lynn and ship out agricultural produce. There were similar trades on the other 'navigations' and they made a major contribution to the prosperity of the county. Business men such as the painter John Constable's father who owned mills on the Stour derived benefits from being able to ship his produce by sea mainly to London. He also invested some of his wealth in coasting vessels.

Local ownership of ships was a notable feature in the ports of the county. In the seventeenth century Ipswich was noted for its fleet of large colliers in the trade of supplying London from the North Eastern collieries. By 1724, Daniel Defoe recorded that the town had lost its hold on the trade to Great Yarmouth; nevertheless there were still forty Ipswich cats with an average tonnage of around 300 tons – much bigger than the usual coasters. Ipswich also owned single-masted hoys that plied between London and the town carrying much the same cargoes as the later Thames barges. The smaller ports also owned ships. As late as 1865, there were twelve schooners owned at Woodbridge, eight at Aldeburgh and four at Orford, but all under 150 tons.

Local ownership was also quite widespread. A master mariner or a merchant might manage a vessel but there were often many small shareholders including farmers and tradesmen. Nor was trade confined to coasting; there were voyages to the Baltic (especially for timber) and to the Mediterranean with salted fish, often with return cargoes of currants or fresh fruit for the London markets.

Local investment in ships also saw the development of a flourishing shipbuilding industry. Ipswich was pre-eminent in the eighteenth century and the reputation of its shipbuilders was such that they attracted orders from the Royal Navy and the East India Co. Lowestoft with its rise as a fishing port built hundreds of wooden fishing smacks and steam drifters. In the twentieth century it supported two shipyards, turning out steel hulled trawlers and small naval vessels. Although Suffolk was a predominantly rural county, the Industrial Revolution and the technologies of iron and steam had a considerable impact on its maritime commerce. Steam tugs made possible shorter and safer passages for sailing ships. Steam paddle steamers opened faster connections with London and the Continent. Steam pile drivers and other advances in civil engineering made it possible to build massive new port facilities at Lowestoft where there was none before 1827 and at Ipswich in 1842 where the biggest dock in Britain was created. Steam trains, which arrived at Ipswich in 1846 and Lowestoft in 1847 with later extensions to Woodbridge, Aldeburgh and Southwold, provided competition to coasters and at the same time opened up inland markets for fresh fish.

Fishing had been a major coastal occupation at least as far back as the Middle Ages when some taxes were paid in salted fish. The fisheries were not only local and inshore; the doggers and busses of Ipswich, Aldeburgh, Southwold and the adjacent villages would sail for Iceland every year to catch cod. While Aldeburgh continued to send a few cod smacks to Iceland until the end of the nineteenth century, the autumn herring fishery grew in size. In the sixteenth and seventeenth centuries this had been dominated by Dutch boats. English ports took an increasing part from the eighteenth century and Lowestoft and its Norfolk rival Great Yarmouth built up large fleets of drifters as well as attracting large number of boats from Scotland. Much of the catch was salted and smoked and exported. The invention of a steam net-hauling capstan by

Elliott & Garood of Beccles in 1884 improved catching capacity. The first stem drifter, the *Consolation* of 1897, was built at Lowestoft for George Catchpole of Kessingland. When other local owners saw how successful the *Consolation* was, they followed Catchpole's lead. Sailing drifters were quickly discarded and by 1913 there were 350 steamers and only a few sailing boats. Lowestoft also developed a mid-water fleet of trawlers which thrived after the rapid decline in the drifter's catches in the 1920s. Many were locally built and when their prosperity began to slide in the 1970s, quite a few were converted into support or safety vessels for the new North Sea offshore oil and gas industry. At the time of writing, the last remnants of this fleet are likely to disappear with the European Common Fishery proposals to close much of the North Sea to allow fish stocks a chance to replenish. There are still inshore fishing boats and many, though motorised, still retain the hull shape of the traditional local beach lugger design.

The Suffolk coast with its treacherous shifting sand banks, difficult harbour entrance and the power of the North Sea gales was always dangerous for sailing ships. There were huge numbers of vessels passing the coast from the late seventeenth century because it was on the coastal route to London. There were many accidents and wrecks often with a huge loss of life. In 1770, some thirty ships ran ashore with 200 drownings all in one night. Until 1801, there was no lifeboat service although there were beach companies who were dedicated to salvage and supplying passing vessels. In that year a subscription was raised to build and station a lifeboat at Lowestoft and another at Bawdsey at the entrance to the Deben. This initiative evolved into the Suffolk Humane Society in 1806. More lifeboat stations were established at other coastal settlements. While there were now means of saving lives from shipwrecked vessels, shipping casualties could still be heavy. James Maggs of Southwold wrote in his diary for 3 November 1855: 'While the gale was at its height, the *Hylton Castle* and the *Emma*, both of Sunderland; the *Ocean* and *Cape Horn* of Whitby; and the *Nelson* of South Shields were driven ashore but the crews saved.' In 1858, local efforts were merged with the Royal National Lifeboat Institution which continues to this day. The brave crews that voluntarily manned the lifeboats should also not be forgotten especially those who lost their lives such as seven lost on the *Aldeburgh* in 1899.

Widespread leisure boating developed in the nineteenth century. At first, it was the pursuit of the wealthy, who could afford to build large cutters and pay crews (often local fishermen) to man them. However, sailing regattas with all kinds of sailing and rowing races attracted large audiences. Oulton Broad was a favourite and the building of the railway to Lowestoft brought in many more spectators. This era also saw the establishment of yacht clubs to organise races and social events. Sailing became gradually more democratic with the rise of smaller 'one-design' day sailing yachts and these in turn led to dinghy racing which mushroomed in popularity after the Second World War. Reliable internal combustion engines made it possible for anyone to take to the inland waters of the River Waveney with its connection to the Norfolk Broads. Local boatbuilders, such as Robertsons and Whisstocks at Woodbridge, were able to build up a reputation for launching fine yachts. The huge numbers of moorings that cover large areas of the county's estuaries are a reflection of the continuing popularity of yachting.

The older Suffolk ports such as Aldeburgh, Southwold, Orford and Woodbridge have lost all their commercial trade. Ipswich and Lowestoft continue to operate but they are overshadowed by a new port, Felixstowe. This was a privately-owned and under-used tidal dock which could only accommodate coasters. In 1951, it was sold to H.G. Parker, a local corn merchant, who refurbished the dock to take bigger vessels and added an oil terminal and a roll-on roll-off ferry berth. In 1964, he and his board embarked on expanding the port as a full-scale container terminal for deep sea ships. This soon attracted business away from more traditionally run ports such as Tilbury. It, along with Southampton, is the premier container port of the kingdom and the deep water of the Orwell estuary means that it accommodates the latest and largest vessels. At the time of writing, its Hong Kong-based owners are about to expand its annual capacity by another 1.5 million 20ft containers. So, the shipping scene in Suffolk continues to change and is a long way from the glorious days of sail and fishing drifters. Today's vessels are container ships, ferries and yachts.

# *One*
# Early Shipping

This carnelian gem stone from a Roman ring was found at Caistor St Edmunds near Norwich. Venta Icenorum, the town here, would have been in water communication with Burgh Castle, the Roman fort on the Suffolk side of the Yare-Waveney estuary. It shows a Roman sailing vessel approaching a lighthouse. It has a main mast with a square sail and a second sail on the artemon or bowsprit projecting over the bow. The double line of strokes at the bottom of the ship could be interpreted as either waves or possible double-banked oars. If it is the latter, then this might be one of the warships based at Burgh Castle.

The massive walls of Burgh Castle are standing witnesses of the Roman's commitment to coastal defence in the third and fourth centuries. In the course of time the raiders became settlers and the Anglo-Saxon kingdom of East Anglia had replaced Roman government. By the sixth century Burgh Castle became the base for the Christian missionary St Fursey. Apart from its isolation Burgh Castle, which appealed to Irish monks, like the saint it was well placed for travelling by boat either inland or along the coast.

ROMAN RECREATION AT BURGH CASTLE

The local naturalist Arthur Patterson had a humorous idea of what the Romans might have been doing when not patrolling the coast.

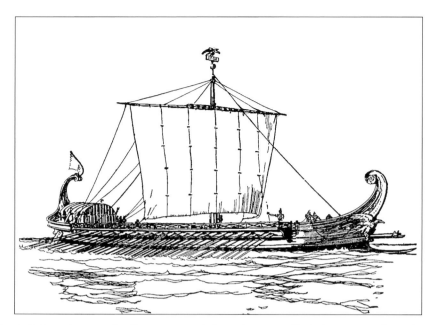

The *Classis Britannica* was the Roman naval fleet that patrolled the east and south coasts to intercept the increasing number of raiding boats of Angles, Saxons and Jutes. They were rowing galleys. Most had two banks of oars although one trireme with three banks was recorded.

The Sutton Hoo ship can be dated to the early seventh century. The superbly wrought and valuable 'grave goods' showed this was the burial of an exceptionally important person. A probable candidate was Raedwald (*c*.596–625) who ruled East Anglia and was 'overlord' of the English kings from 616. The ship was 89ft (27m) long and 15ft (4.5m) wide, and was dragged up from the River Deben. It was covered by a large mound of earth, possibly with the high bow and stern still visible.

*Right:* The Sutton Hoo ship is not the first Anglo-Saxon ship to be found in Suffolk. The Snape ship burial (dating from *c.*640 AD) was excavated in 1862 but little detail of the ship itself was recorded. The Sutton Hoo ship was first excavated in 1939 and re-excavated to gather further details in the 1960s. The wooden planking of the hull had disappeared, leaving an outline in the sandy soil along with the iron rivets that fastened the hull together.

*Below:* This picture shows the final part of the 1966 excavation campaign where the archaeologists made a plaster cast of the hull. The lines of iron rivets are clearly visible on the right.

*Above:* A half-size version of the Sutton Hoo ship has been built to test its characteristics. It has proved a seaworthy design and has handled well under sail as well as oars. However, there is no evidence of a mast on the original. At present it is displayed at the excellent new Sutton Hoo Visitor Centre which includes a full-size reconstruction of the grave compartment.

*Left:* King Athelstan I of East Anglia (c.827 - c.841) issued a silver penny illustrating a ship on its obverse. This was found at West Harling just over the Norfolk boundary in 1978. It depicts a type of sailing vessel known as a hulc with a rounded hull, a single mast and sail and no oars. It is possible that Ipswich merchants of the time used hulcs in their trade across the North Sea to the Rhineland.

There have been no finds of complete medieval ships in Suffolk. Two side rudders have been trawled up in a valley now lost to the sea. An Anglo-Saxon log boat was later found nearby. There are also fragments of medieval vessels buried in Buss Creek, near Southwold, which await excavation.

Stuart Bacon is a leading figure in Suffolk underwater archaeology, especially for his work on the lost port of Dunwich. He maintains a fascinating visitor centre on this important work in his craft shop at Orford. He also has several timbers that probably come from eighteenth or nineteenth-century ships displayed in front of his shop.

Dunwich was probably the most flourishing of the medieval ports of Suffolk. It was a self-governing borough and the official seal depicted the main source of prosperity: ships. This seal of 1199 shows a clinker-built sailing ship equipped with two fighting castles and a fighting top up the mast. Note the large side rudder for steering. Whether the fish in the sea were meant to show it was a fishing boat is a matter of opinion.

A later seal for Dunwich dating from 1346 depicts a different design of craft, the hulc, which we have already seen depicted on Athelstan's coin. This was still a common type of merchant ship. The single mast and sail has been replaced by a portrait of King Edward III. Little is known about this type of ship. There have been no wreck finds. It also appears on the seal of Orford and there are three hulcs on Ipswich's coat of arms.

The cog was another common type of medieval merchant ship. It originated in Scandinavia, possibly as early as the seventh century. It was flat-bottomed with clinker-built sides. By the thirteenth century it was a large decked merchant ship with a rudder fixed to the stern post and with 'castles' at the bow and stern integrated into the hull rather than temporary after-thoughts. The seal of Ipswich from 1200 shows such a cog.

A complete cog was found in the River Weser in 1962 and has been conserved at the German National Maritime at Bremerhaven. Several replicas have been built. This was the first and is seen here on an experimental trip to Roskilde in Denmark with a replica of Viking cargo ship alongside.

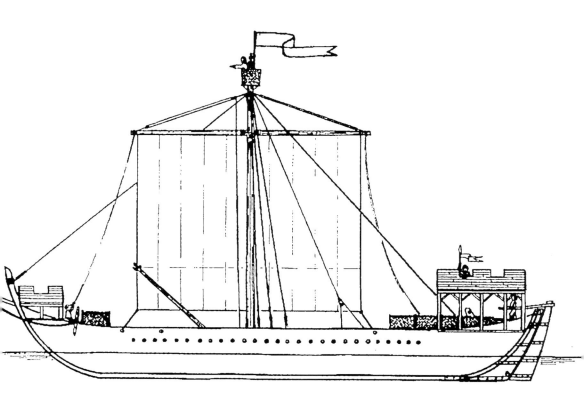

In 1294 Edward II ordered the building of twenty war galleys from different ports, including one each from Dunwich and Ipswich. The accounts for the one ordered from Newcastle have survived and show that these ships must have been among the largest of the period. They were about 120ft (36.5m) long and 18ft (5.5m) wide. They could be rowed as well as sailed and, although the specification required 120 rowers, it is difficult to see how they could all be fitted in unless they double-banked like a Roman galley; a more likely figure would be sixty. Medieval naval tactics consisted mainly of manoeuvring alongside an enemy vessel to allow the large complement of soldiers to board her. This illustration is a reconstruction of the Newcastle galley and it is likely that Suffolk ones were fairly close to this design.

*Opposite, below:* This carving of the Ark is to be found on the tomb of Henry Fitzroy, Duke of Richmond of 1636, in Framlingham church. The hull appears to be based on a merchant vessel with a forecastle and poop fully integrated into the hull and possibly with clinker planking. This overlapping technique persisted in quite large coasting vessels known as 'billy-boys' into the middle of the nineteenth century.

*Above left:* Fishing, especially the Icelandic cod fishery and autumn herring fishery, was of immense importance. In the fifteenth century Dunwich, Walberswick and Aldeburgh owned 'great boats' of up to 80 tons and two masts that fished for cod with long lines with hundreds of baited hooks. The smaller villages such as Covehithe and Kessingland caught herring and sprats with drift nets using boats (batella) about 20ft (6m) long.

*Above right:* The fifteenth century also witnessed the development of larger merchant ships influenced by Mediterranean shipbuilding practice with heavy frames, carvel planking, large superstructures at bow and stern, and two or three masts. These carracks proved capable of long-distance voyages. They have a Suffolk connection since one of them was depicted on the town badge of Aldeburgh and you can still see one carved into the mantelpiece of the Moot Hall there.

Smaller sixteenth and seventeenth-century coasting vessels had one or two masts and various rigs including a sprit mainsail, which is still the predominant feature of the rigging of a modern Thames barge. These two examples have been sketched from a pictorial map of Aldeburgh drawn by Ananias Appleton in 1588. This is striking because it also shows four galleons off the shore, another eight in the River Alde, along with twenty-three small fishing boats. A similar map of Great Yarmouth shows a very similar range of ship types which tends to confirm the authenticity of the Aldeburgh one.

*Opposite:* The sixteenth-century galleon was a refinement of the earlier carrack. The modern replica of Sir Francis Drake's exploration vessel, the *Golden Hind*, gives an excellent idea of their appearance. They had square sail (the sprit sail) below the bowsprit and two sails on the fore and main masts and a triangular lateen sail on the mizzen. Captain Bartholomew Gosnold of Grundisburgh, near Woodbridge, commanded the *Godspeed* across the Atlantic to explore the Virginia coast in 1602. In 1606 he returned with a party of settlers to found Jamestown in 1607. The open air museum on the site of this early settlement includes a replica of the *Godspeed*. Her plans do not exist but it was possible to work out her dimensions from her tonnage and the well-established mathematical formulae that were used by seventeenth-century shipwrights.

This seventeenth-century oil painting was discovered under fifteen layers of wallpaper in the Jolly Sailor inn at Orford. It depicts three late seventeenth-century two-deck warships of the Royal Navy. It is supposed to represent the Battle of Sole Bay which was fought against the Dutch – our mercantile rivals – in 1672. On the other hand it could be an early example of a common form of composition in marine painting which shows one vessel in two or three different positions.

The Red Lion at Mendlesham, near Woodbridge, has a genuine seventeenth-century naval figurehead. Carvings of lions were a standard design for larger warships of the time. Just how it came to decorate this old pub is a mystery but it could be linked to one of the two naval battles with the Dutch – Lowestoft in 1665 and Sole Bay in 1672.

Seventeenth-century Ipswich was noted for building operating large cargo ships of 300 tons and more in the coal trade between the collieries of Durham and Northumberland and London. The expanding capital had an insatiable demand for fuel. By 1724, when Daniel Defoe visited the town, Great Yarmouth had pushed Ipswich out of the top place. Nevertheless forty 'cats' were still locally owned, only returning to their home port for repairs or laying up in the winter.

While the cats may have declined in the eighteenth century, Ipswich remained a busy port and this can be seen in the engraving by the Buck brothers and also John Cleveley's panorama of the Ipswich quays in 1753 in Ipswich Museum. Both feature a large number of single-masted gaff-rigged vessels known as hoys, which were similar to this model of a hoy.

This painting by William Anderson, one of the foremost marine artists of the late eighteenth century, shows the River Orwell near Ipswich in 1797. A Dutch barge, a tjalk and a brig are drifting up on the tide with very little or no wind. Contrary wind or calms could prolong short coastal voyages from days to weeks. Note the hoy tied up at the windmill's quay.

Kirby's 'Correct map of the Suffolk Coast' of 1736 shows two of the smaller eighteenth-century types of boat. One appears to be a fishing buss with square sails and a two-masted gaff-rigged boat which may be an Orwell wherry. These were noted passenger ferries but no one is quite sure how they were rigged. Certainly they had more in common with the passenger-carrying wherries of the Thames than the more burdensome cargo wherries of the Norfolk Broads.

# *Two*
# Barges and Wherries

A Thames barge enters Southwold harbour during the time of its reconstruction in 1906 to 1907. The bowsprit has been heaved up, the topsail halliards let go and the main sail partly brailed in. The mate is forward, ready to lower the foresail to take more 'way' off her once through the entrance.

The *Venture* under main and top sails glides through Ipswich lock at high tide. She was built by Shrubsalls at Ipswich in 1910 and was working under sail alone in 1959.

A second view of the *Venture* as she makes her way to Cranfield's mill at the head of the dock.

The same time, but a contrast in rigs. The barge *Jock* on the left is a motor barge with two scraps of sails, the *Venture* is all sail and the *Beatrice Maud* on the right has a motor but retains her mainsail with its sprit but has no top mast.

Ipswich Lock outward bound with a contrast in sterns. The *Unity* (1862), the barge in the centre, is one of older types with a large rib-breaking tiller instead of a wheel for steering. The *Carrie Louise* (1890) with a counter stern is a boomie barge, gaff rigged instead of the usual sprit. The big barge on the left is the *Malvina* built at Frindsbury in 1890, registered at Rochester and owned in Ipswich.

A billy-boy at anchor in Southwold harbour, c.1900. Billy-boys originated from the Humber, its tributaries and Lincolnshire. They were bluff in the bow and the older ones were clinker built. Their design may have descended from medieval vessels. They frequently carried square sail on their main masts.

Older types of rig needed a bigger crew than a Thames barge which could be managed by two men. The rig could be set in various configurations according to the circumstances and there were winches to assist with setting and hauling them in. The *Repertor* is a late example and was built with a steel hull just across the Essex border at Mistley in 1921.

The shallow draft of the Thames barge also made it ideal for entering shallow river entrances such as the River Deben at Bawdsey. They are fitted with lifting keels known as lee boards to ensure they sail efficiently. *Pudge's* port lee board is clearly visible in its hauled up position in the previous picture.

*Opposite, above:* Snape was one of the most difficult places to reach because it lay up the winding channel of the River Alde above Aldeburgh. There was a pilot on hand to advise because the winding channel was so difficult. There was a large maltings at the head of navigation.

*Opposite, below:* Thames barges still come to Snape and at present the little *Cygnet* is based there. She was built at Frindsbury, Essex, in 1881 and is only 13 gross tons. She was designed to carry farm produce and finished up working on the Stour and the Orwell.

Woodbridge was another busy upriver barge port in the late nineteenth century. Two spritsail barges lie off the quay below the Tide Mill while a boomie barge drifts on the tide with scarcely any wind to fill the sails.

Southwold in 1906 or 1907 with the big barge *Alaric* (73 tons) in the foreground. She was built in 1901 at Sandwich, Kent, and was owned by the London & Rochester Shipping Co.

*Right:* Thames barges still sail in Suffolk waters. The *Ena* (73 tons) seen off Felixstowe in 1995 was built at Harwich in 1906 for R&W Paul of Ipswich. Their barges always carried a distinctive white cross on their top sails.

*Below:* The *May* (1891), *Spinaway C* (1899) and *Tollesbury* (1901) were all working Ipswich barges in 1959. All three have survived although the *Spinaway C* is being rebuilt and the *Tollesbury* is a restaurant vessel in Millwall Dock.

Thames barges share many similar features with Dutch sailing barges but lack their distinctive hull shape with bluff bows and tumblehome (the in-turning part of the upper part of the hull). Trading links between the Netherlands and Suffolk go back to the Middle Ages and Dutch-owned coasting barges were seen in Suffolk ports.

*Opposite, above:* The *Marjorie* was built in 1902 at Ipswich and maintained by R&W Paul at their Dock End yard. The last barge to be built there was the *Ardwina* in 1916.

*Opposite, below:* The *Thalatta* was built in 1906 at Harwich and was re-rigged as a boomie. In 1948, when owned by R&W Paul, she was reduced to a motor barge with only a foresail.

The *Thalatta* has been restored as a Mulie barge with a gaff-rigged mizzen mast. Today she provides sail training for young people.

*Opposite, above:* Pin Mill on the south bank of the Orwell has remained a centre for barge repair. The famous racing barge *Phoenecian*, which won four Thames and Medway Barge Races between 1931 and 1936, underwent extensive repairs in the 1990s here after being based at Ipswich for many years.

*Opposite, below:* The full restoration was completed at Maldon, Essex, which is her new base. Thames barges, especially those with wooden hulls, need constant and expensive maintenance. The *Phoenecian* is a relatively young barge and was launched at Sittingbourne, Kent, in 1922. Note the *Thalatta* alongside her.

Not all barges have survived to be rebuilt. Many were taken out of trading and converted into house boats. Their roomy holds without obstructions made them ideal. Unfortunately many were in poor condition and were eventually abandoned. The *Leslie West* built at Gravesend in 1900 is one of several abandoned barges at Pin Mill.

The *Maid of Connaught* of 1899 – turned into a barge yacht in 1960 after years of work for the Leigh Building Supply Co. – is another Pin Mill hulk. Recently, the hull of the steel barge *Mermaid* has been hauled out for restoration by the local boatbuilder.

*Pages 40 and 41*: Suffolk was also a county with inland water transport. The River Waveney was navigable as far as Bungay before 1650. By 1670, silting prevented barges getting above Beccles and in that year an Act of Parliament was obtained to build three locks to re-open navigation to Bungay. It remained an important highway for transporting coal, timber and agricultural produce until declining traffic was forced on its owners Watney, Combe & Reid, maltsers, in 1934.

ELLINGHAM MILL

ELLINGHAM LOCK

DANIEL MILLS'S LOCK

DITCHINGHAM
MALTING &
BREWERY

WAINFORD
LOCK

MALTING

WEIR

THE 'ALBION' AT
BUNGAY STAITHE

BUNGAY

BUNGAY STAITHE

NEAR BUNGAY

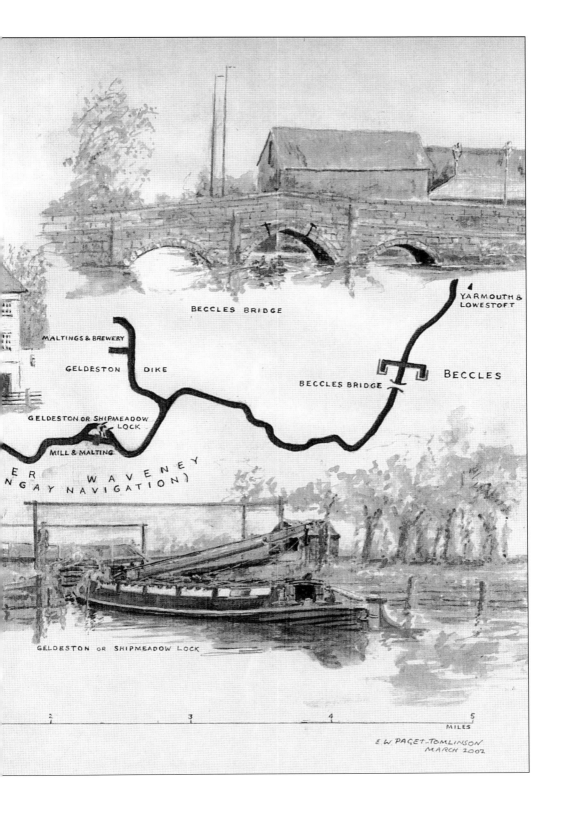

BECCLES BRIDGE

YARMOUTH &
LOWESTOFT

MALTINGS & BREWERY

GELDESTON DIKE

BECCLES BRIDGE

BECCLES

GELDESTON or SHIPMEADOW
LOCK

MILL & MALTING

ER          WAVENEY
NGAY NAVIGATION)

GELDESTON OR SHIPMEADOW LOCK

2          3          4          5
MILES

E.W. PAGET-TOMLINSON
MARCH 2002

Traffic on the Waveney was carried first in sailing keels which were square rigged and later (probably from the late eighteenth century) in wherries. These were clinker-built, double-ended barges with a tall single mast and black tanned gaff sail. The mast had a large lead counterweight at its foot which allowed it to be lowered easily when passing through fixed bridges.

*Opposite, below:* Beccles was an important inland port which was served not only by wherries, like the one on the right of the picture, but also by steam tugs and coasters such as Thames barges and billy-boys.

Geldeston (or Shipmeadow) Lock was the first of three locks that extended navigation on the Waveney to thriving market town of Bungay – a centre for malting locally grown barley. That famous survivor, the wherry *Albion*, was built there in 1898. Wherries were obliged to lower their masts when in the lock and you can see one in this picture waiting for the water to be lowered. Note also the rowing skiffs for hire to the left of the lock.

Wherries also plied on the River Blyth between Southwold and Halesworth; it was a nine-mile navigation with four locks promoted by a Halesworth brewer in 1757 and opened in 1761. It saw little use after 1850 and the last wherry called in about 1906. The warehouse at Halesworth was witness of a once thriving trade but with only two leisure boats in sight.

*Opposite, above:* The *Yare* was a wooden dumb barge built in 1890 for work on the River Gipping between Ipswich and Bramford. It has been converted into a smart house boat at Pin Mill.

*Opposite, below:* The Ipswich & Stowmarket Navigation (the River Gipping) was navigable in the Middle Ages, and Caen stone for the building of the great abbey church at Bury St Edmunds passed that way. It was much improved in the 1790s with new locks and many of the river bend straightened out. It continued in use into the twentieth century with Fison's and Packard's, who both made fertilizers using steam barges which towed two dumb barges as in this picture taken near Bramford.

Lowestoft was the sea terminus of the Norwich & Lowestoft Navigation opened in 1832. This created a harbour entrance and then used the Rivers Waveney and Yare with a connecting canal – the New Cut – at Haddiscoe to make Norwich accessible to sea-going vessels. The four wherries in the picture lie in the Inner Harbour at Lowestoft. The two in the front appear to be rigged for local harbour traffic as they have light masts possibly for a small lug sail rather than full-size wherry sail.

# Three

# Sailing Ships of the Eighteenth and Nineteenth Centuries

Ipswich's shipbuilders had had a reputation for building good-quality wooden sailing ships including warships. This fine-lined brig – probably for the Mediterranean trade – was on the launching ways in 1858 at the St Clement's shipyard.

West Indiamen were a more common product of the early nineteenth-century shipbuilders of Ipswich. These were often three-masted barques, a more economical rig than a full-rigged ship, and were in the 300-400 ton range.

*Above:* Smaller square-rigged vessels were more common products of the Suffolk shipyards, which were to be found not only at Ipswich but at Woodbridge, Aldeburgh, Southwold and Lowestoft. The brig *Berbice* was built at Lowestoft in 1816 for the Mediterranean trade and owned in Southwold.

*Right:* This charming early Victorian figurehead displayed in the Southwold Museum probably came from a vessel in the Mediterranean trade because she holds a bunch of grapes. Suffolk vessels would load barrels of salted herring on the outward voyage and return with grapes, currants, oranges and lemons.

# CHARLES T. TOWNSEND,

## CUSTOM-HOUSE, SHIP, AND GENERAL AGENT;

### HALL OF COMMERCE,

## IPSWICH.

Vice-Consul for Sweden and Norway.

Suffolk ports also enjoyed a good volume of trade with Scandinavia and visiting ships needed locally based agents to assist with paperwork, obtaining supplies, repairs and return freights. This advertisement was published in *Marwood's Shipping Register & Commercial Advertiser* of 1855.

The *Bergens Handel* (the Bergen Trader) was typical of the early nineteenth-century Norwegian merchant ships and was rigged as a Snow, with a small mast behind the main mast to carry the large gaff rigged sail (the spanker) at the stern.

Other foreign ships were frequent visitors to Suffolk ports, especially Dutch-owned vessels. In Ipswich in about 1860, there was a Dutch galliot with the *Fanny* of Ipswich (built at Gainsborough in 1827) and a brigantine astern.

Ketches were fore and aft rigged with a main mast and a shorter mizzen mast and were fairly rare when this specimen was photographed off Cobbold's shipyard in 1858.

Brigs were employed in large numbers in the north-east coal trade. The majority were built and owned in Newcastle or Sunderland, served London and passed the Suffolk coast on their voyages to and from the Thames.

After the 1860s an increasing number of sailing ships were built of wrought iron and later steel as the costs of these materials decreased and the techniques of using them improved. The topsail schooner *Stirling*, photographed at Lowestoft, was built in Holland in 1897 for her Barton-on-Humber owners.

The fierce North Sea gales and the dangerous lee shore accounted for many similar casualties in the collier fleet. This painting recalls a winter gale in 1881 when no less than thirty ships were put ashore around Lowestoft.

The Ipswich Shipwrecked Seamen's Society was formed in 1826 to assist local sailors who had suffered loss and hardship. It continued for over a century and this picture shows one of the anniversary parades of the 1920s.

Local coasting brigs, such as this example photographed at Ipswich in the late 1850s, were not built for speed but for cargo capacity. They were typically bluff in the bow and deep drafted in relation to their length.

*Pages 56 and 57:* Lowestoft harbour in the 1890s still received small numbers of square riggers. Here, one of the Great Eastern Railway's paddle tugs, possibly the *Rainbow* of 1864, has charge of a deeply laden barquentine and is about to pass the new swing bridge of 1896. To the left fishing smacks' masts can just be seen in the Fish Dock and to the left lie the elegant yachts of the Norfolk and Suffolk Yacht Club with a steam yacht lying on the quay, normally reserved for the tugs of the port.

*Right:* The same hull form was also found on the top sail schooners which succeeded them. This small schooner was on the mud being scrubbed and tarred at Ipswich in 1859. The long exposure needed has blurred the men working on the hull.

*Below:* The brigantine *William Parker* was built at Wells, Norfolk, in 1840 and owned in Ipswich between 1857 and 1892. It is photographed alongside the grand Custom House of Ipswich.

Inner Harbour Entrance Lowestoft W.1614.

Woodbridge was also a schooner port and in 1865 twelve small schooners, all of under 100 tons, were owned there. This later picture shows a top-sail schooner at the quay with a Thames barge converted to house boat.

Deep-sea sailing ships continued to arrive at Ipswich with cargoes of American or Australian wheat well into the 1930s. They had to anchor in Butterman's Bay below Ipswich while Thames barges lightered part of their cargo so that they could enter Ipswich Dock. The ship *Westgate* of 1885 was discharging the rest of her cargo of wheat and barley there in April 1914.

# *Four*
# Steam and Motor Ships

Steam 'packets' became a regular part of the coastal trade from the 1820s. Early vessels were invariably paddlers, usually with low-pressure boilers and side lever engines. They used large quantities of coal which reduced their cargo capacity. The Ipswich Steam Navigation Co. was formed in 1824 to provide a service to London.

*Above:* Steam on the River Orwell in about 1870. This evocative picture showed how much and how little had been changed by the development of the steam engine. The rural approaches to the port were intact but in the twentieth century would be developed with new quays and a power station. But the paddle tug leaves a long trail of black smoke and in the background there are two tall chimneys as symbols of the town's growing industries.

*Below:* Railway competition took over most of the coastal passenger trade by the 1840s. Three passenger-carrying paddle steamers – the *Suffolk, Essex* (1895) and *Norfolk* (1900) – continued to ply between Ipswich and Harwich with calls at Pin Mill and Shotley, and were owned by the Great Eastern Railway Co.

Coastal excursions also flourished and the *Walton Belle* was one of the Belle fleet that ran a regular summer service from the Thames to Great Yarmouth.

The Belle steamers called at Southwold pier. This popular trip was recollected in 2002 when the paddle steamer *Waverley* docked at Southwold's newly restored pier.

*Above:* Lowestoft was not only a port but a seaside resort and there were regular paddle steamer excursions both inland to Oulton Broad and the River Waveney, and to and from Great Yarmouth just up the coast. This is either the *Lord Nelson* or the *Lord Nelson* entering Lowestoft from Great Yarmouth in 1902.

*Left:* The port of Lowestoft was substantially improved by the railway contractor Samuel Morton Peto from 1844 onwards. He hoped to see regular steamer services to continental ports to build up the railway traffic. In the event, Lowestoft lost out to Harwich and found salvation as a major fishing port. Paddle steamers as tugs rather than as North Sea ferries remained a crucial part of the port's services for the growing fishing industry.

Perhaps the paddle steamer's role as a specialist tug was of greater importance in the longer term than the packet services. Paddle tugs enabled sailing ships to enter and leave port with greater regularity and safety. Paddle tugs also provided salvage services and sometimes towed sailing-pulling lifeboats out to sea. The tug *Imperial* was under repair in the dry dock at Lowestoft. This dock was opened in 1856 and was an important legacy of the bankrupt North of Europe Steam Navigation Co.

Lowestoft tugs were owned by the Great Eastern Railway Co. which owned the harbour. They were stationed at the entrance to the yacht basin. The three here appear to be the *Imperial*, *Rainbow* and the *Powerful*.

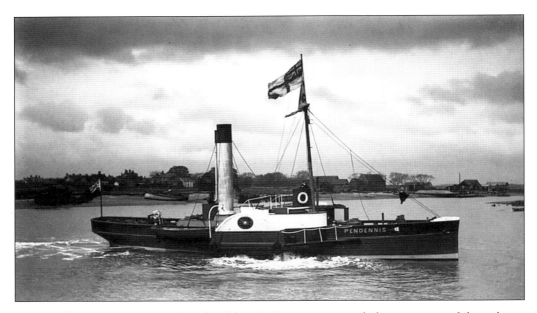

The paddle tug *Pendennis* at Southwold, *c.*1910, was stationed there to assist fishing boats coming to land their catches of herring during the autumn fishery.

Screw-propelled steamers became common from the 1850s after the successful experiments of the previous decade. They needed high-pressure boilers and fast-running engines. This half model at Butt and Oyster Inn at Pin Mill has the proportions of one of these early screw steamers. Its identity seems to be a mystery.

The *Vic 56*, outward bound from the Orwell, was a Second World War standard design of coasting steamer with a single hold and engines aft. It is a reminder of the small steam barges that plied between various Suffolk ports and London. For example, the malting firm Garrett's of Snape ran the *Katherine* and the *Gladys* delivering their product to London breweries.

The classic steam coaster came into its own from the 1890s with its steering position amidships, engines aft and two holds served by cargo derricks on two masts. This specimen was pictured at Southwold, c.1910. Similar vessels were to be found at Ipswich and Lowestoft as late as the 1950s

Coastal steamers with the older lay-out of engines and boilers amidships which concentrated the weight in the centre hull remained popular with some companies such as France, Fenwick & Co. Their ships were frequently seen steaming past the Suffolk coast en route for London. The *Ribbleton* was not one of their fleet but typifies the design with holds on either side of the midship engines and crew accommodation.

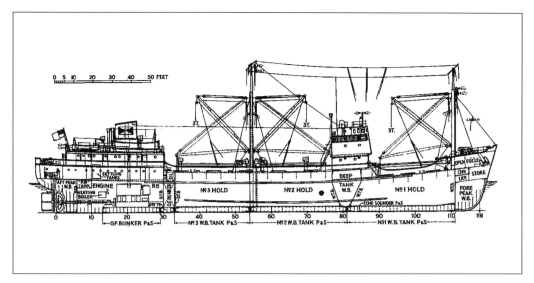

Coasters with the bridge amidships continued to be built after the Second World War. They were invariably equipped with diesel engines, which had become reliable and economical and reduced the number of crew needed in the engine room. This design of 1,500 ton motor coaster was built at Goole and Grangemouth from 1950 to 1957 for Everard's.

F.T. Everard of Greenhithe on the Thames Estuary started as barge owners and took up motor ships in the 1920s. Their ships such as the *Alfred Everard* of 1957 (1,543 gross tons) were also regular callers at Suffolk ports.

Modern coasting vessels seen in the Orwell estuary are often much larger than their predecessors. Some are of versatile design with heavy cranes that handle either containers or bulk cargoes. Deck space is maximised for carrying containers with the bridge accommodation squashed right at the stern.

*Opposite, above:* The *Iberian Ocean* berthed at Ipswich Dock is a typical 'low air draught' coaster built in 1978 with a cargo capacity of about 1,300 tons. This popular modern design has a single box hold, low superstructure with folding masts for passing under fixed bridges, and no cargo gear.

*Opposite, below:* The *Pamela Everard* was typical of Everard's later ships. She could carry over 2,000 tons of cargo and was built by Richards at Lowestoft in 1984. This view on deck was taken on passage to Ipswich with a cargo of Swedish timber in the 1990s.

Oil products such as petrol have been distributed to coastal fuel depots by sea and are one of the key coastal trades today. Everard's tanker *Authenticity*, built in 1979 at Goole, was off Pin Mill outward bound from a delivery to Ipswich in 1997.

The tanker *Thames Fisher* is one of James Fisher & Son's fleet that can be seen in the Orwell. Built in 1997, she can carry almost 5,000 tons of cargo – a far cry from the tiny sailing colliers that delivered energy in the form of coal in the nineteenth century.

Roll-on roll-off ships (usually shortened to RoRo) are designed to carry wheeled cargo and were developed from the tank landing craft deployed in the invasion of Europe in 1944. Ipswich has developed a RoRo facility in the deep water at the West Quay.

Large RoRos, such as this vessel owned by the Danish Maersk Line, are about the maximum size of vessel to navigate the Orwell. The narrow deep channel is also surrounded by numerous yacht moorings.

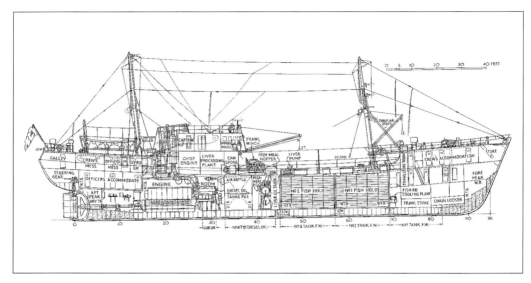

Lowestoft shipbuilders – Richards Ironworks and Brooke Marine – built a wide range of ships. Fishing trawlers were a staple product, but they also built tugs, coasters and other types of service vessels for owners at home and abroad. Brooke Marine also specialised in fast patrol boats, but one of their most novel orders was for twenty trawlers for Russia starting with the launch of the *Pioner* in 1956, at the time of the Cold War.

Other specialised cargo ships seen along the shores of Suffolk have included the crushed-stone carrier *Telnes* of 4,281 gross tons. The large pipe on deck is part of an elaborate conveyor system which can load or discharge the cargo at a rate of up to 1,200 tonnes an hour.

Today very few ships are owned in Suffolk ports. Klyne Tugs of Lowestoft are one example of a local firm that goes from strength to strength. They specialise in supplying powerful tugs such as the *Anglian Prince* for work in the offshore oil and gas industry. She was built in 1980 in China and has four diesel engines geared to two propellers, giving a top speed of 17 knots.

The *Anglian Prince* is on charter (hired out) as an emergency towing vessel to the Maritime & Coastal Agency. In 1996, she was being dry docked at Chatham for routine maintenance. Note how she dwarfs the tug that is assisting with the docking.

The most dramatic change in the county's shipping scene is the rise of the port of Felixstowe. This vies with Southampton as the country's top container port and receives the biggest container ships in the world. The tug *Bentley* is using her 3,800 brake horse power to assist the Chinese container ship *Tsingma Bradge*.

The *Tsingma Bridge* is dwarfed by four massive container cranes which load and discharge her cargo quickly. Containers come in standard 20ft and 40ft lengths and can be carried by ship, road or rail. All the high-value freights, such as electronic goods from the Far East, are packed in containers.

Sealand was the American company that pioneered the container revolution in the 1950s. They were longstanding customers of Felixstowe and their latest ship in 1993 was the *Sealand Lightning*. Her first master was Ken Owen, an Englishman from Derbyshire. They have since merged with the Danish Maersk Line to form the biggest container ship fleet in the world.

The diversity and world-wide range of services calling at Felixstowe. They include the Swiss company Mediterranean Shipping and the French Delmas Line. The latter runs a service to West Africa and its ships *Morgane* and *Delmas* are equipped with self-discharging cranes for ports where container handling is problematic.

The flag ships of Felixstowe are undoubtedly the 'S' class ships of the Danish Maersk Line. These 91,000-ton monsters are the biggest container ships in the world. Their exact container capacity is a company secret but informed estimates are around the 8,000 mark.

The Swedish Stena Lines HSS ferry *Stena Discovery* is another astonishing sight off the Suffolk coast. This is a catamaran built of aluminium in Finland in 1997 and is powered by four gas turbines. It runs a daily service from Parkeston Quay on the Essex side of the Stour to the Hook of Holland.

## *Five*
# Fishing Boats

The village of Kessingland, just south of Lowestoft, had been an important inshore fishery from the Middle Ages. Its fleet of small open lug-rigged punts were hauled out of the sea by hand capstans like the one just to the left of centre. The fishermen to the right are leaning against a net barrow loaded with a drift net.

In winter the shallow waters off Kessingland beach became very dangerous as North Sea gales whipped up the surf into a powerful frenzy. Launching and returning to the beach needed experience and seamanship.

FISHING BOAT SHEDS, KESSINGLAND.

Until the development of the holiday trade in the late nineteenth century, Kessingland, like other Suffolk coastal villages, looked to the sea for work. The fishing sheds, which were used to store nets and spare gear, with the net-drying ground were important enough to merit a picture postcard.

78

Further down the coast, Walberswick on the south bank of the River Blyth was another village where an important fishery operated in the Middle Ages. The punt is lying in the Dunwich Creek.

The Suffolk beach boat or punt was a distinctive type of fishing boat found south of Lowestoft especially on the beaches of Southwold and Aldeburgh. They were usually about 18ft (5.5m) long and beamy – 7ft (2.1m) with a good capacity for big catches of herring or sprats. They could be used for trawling or drifting and they rowed as well as sailed.

The size of Southwold's fleet of punts in the early 1900s is evident from this picture taken in the spratting season. The crew of three of the first boat appear to have had a fairly meagre catch with their drift net. Note their waterproof canvas smocks and the variety of headgear.

Another view of Southwold from the same era. Note the large number of boats, some with their sails drying. Southwold like Kessingland had an extensive range of sheds for storing spare gear. The big pile of fish boxes to the right suggests that catches were good. The narrow gauge railway to Southwold which opened in 1879 meant that local fishermen had wider access to markets for selling their catches.

The *Three Sisters* was built at Thorpness to the north of Southwold in 1896. In 1994, she was bought by Robert Simper, the maritime historian and author, and restored to her original sailing rig.

This and the preceding picture taken on the Deben last year demonstrate the impressive sail area of the main dipping lug sail and the standing mizzen. It was customary to tan the sails.

This is an unusual punt because it has a foresail, gaff-rigged sails on the main and the mizzen plus top sails. The main sail is 'loose-footed' like the shrimpers built at Great Yarmouth.

*Opposite, above:* This Cornish lugger *Girl Sybil* (PZ is Penzance) provided day trips at Southwold in 2002. Although the hull form and dimensions are different, she is a reminder of the large decked herring luggers that were based at Lowestoft and Southwold in the mid-nineteenth century.

*Opposite, below:* From the 1920s the design of the punt was modified to take an engine. The first engines were of a low horsepower and the sails were often retained. Frank Knight's yard at Woodbridge was still building them in after the Second World War. However, today their numbers have declined in favour of more modern designs. The *Sheree Ann* of Lowestoft on Aldeburgh beach is built along traditional lines but features a wheelhouse with radar and a stern gallows for trawling.

SOUTHWOLD HARBOUR.

.erring lugger discharging her catch at Southwold, c.1910, on the new quay which wa
igned for the overflow of boats from Lowestoft during the autumn fishery.

*posite, above:* Another example of a modern punt trawling on the River Ore just belov
ord. The Butley River, a tributary of the Ore, has also seen the laying of oyster beds.

*posite, below:* Once the catch of herrings was taken out of the drift nets and stowed in th
d, every boat would try and sail back to port as soon as possible because the first boats usuall
 the best prices. Before the railway arrived at Lowestoft, luggers would come to the beach te
d their herrings quickly.

Two herring drifters warping their way out of Southwold harbour in calm weather. These may b̶e two of the boats that were owned in Walberswick. They are typical of the type with clink̶ b̶uilt hulls and loose-footed main sails. The main mast could be lowered when drift fishing.

The herring market: Lowestoft in the boom time before the First World War. Herring were measured in crans, weighing $3\frac{1}{2}$cwt (179kg), and were landed in special quarter-cran baskets.

Lowestoft and Great Yarmouth might receive as many as a thousand visiting boats at the height of herring fishery. Here the boats are berthed four abreast, with an early steam drifter and three Scottish luggers, known as Zulus.

The first fishing boat to berth at the new facilities at Southwold on 13 June 1907 was the Lowestoft-registered *Amelia*.

Southwold's improvements attracted a substantial Scottish fleet. This forest of masts seems to be all Scottish luggers except for two Thames barges with their distinctive diagonally rigged sprits.

The barges in the last picture were probably delivering empty barrels for the catch. Herring would be gutted and salted on the quay by teams of skilled Scottish fisher girls who came down to East Anglia for the season.

The first steam drifter, the *Consolation*, was built at Lowestoft in 1897. She was little more than a dandy, i.e. a sailing smack with an engine. Within a few years wheelhouses became standard but the main sail was retained. The *Prosperity* was built at Oulton Broad in 1906 for owners at Kessingland, and at 72 gross tons was larger than the earlier sailing smacks.

The steam drifter fleet grew rapidly after 1900 and by 1914 there few sailing drifters left. Most of the new vessels were built locally and many were painted for their proud owners by local marine artists such as E.G. Tench (1880-1940). The *Clara and Alice* was built in 1909 for William Turrell of Lowestoft and has the classic profile of a steam drifter.

*Opposite, above:* Later drifters were larger than their predecessors and were built with steel rather than wooden hulls. Some were also to go trawling after the herring season finished. The *Tritonia* was built at Oulton Broad in 1930. She had a long career because she was converted to a motor trawler and only went for scrap in 1976.

*Opposite, below:* The drifter *Lydia Eva* was saved for preservation by the Maritime Trust in the 1970s. At the moment she is laid up at Lowestoft awaiting major repairs. The wooden drifter *Golden Chance*, built by John Chambers at Lowestoft in 1914, survives as a hulk in the Falkland Islands. She was sent out there as a sealing vessel in 1949.

The tug *Lowestoft* is returning to harbour, having towed a drifter and two sailing trawlers to sea. The one on the right is the *Content*. An early steam drifter with a thin 'Woodbine' funnel is visible to the right of the tug.

The older twin-funnel paddle tug *Rainbow* tows two sailing trawlers to sea in the 1890s. Most fishing vessels were towed out in groups of two or more to save on towage charges.

*Opposite, below:* Trawlers sailing out of Lowestoft in fine weather. This saved the towage charge of 5 shillings per boat. A few sailing trawlers managed to eke out a living into the 1930s. Some were converted to motor vessels or sold to the Faeroe Islands.

The trawler *Ruby* was painted by P. Gregory, a Lowestoft artist, in 1900. Trawlers were larger with more sail for dragging a beam trawl than the drifters. The *Excelsior* has been restored to sailing condition and is based at Lowestoft. She was built there in 1921 and measure 77ft (23.5m) overall with a gross tonnage of 55 tons.

The Fish Dock, Lowestoft: trawlers had to berth head on to the quay because of their numbers. On the right is a trawler registered at Ramsgate and then there are three local vessels: the *Nancy* (date unknown), *Beryl* (1903) and *Lily of Devon* (1900).

Trawling was a hard and dangerous occupation with uncertain rewards. The crew were paid in shares from the proceeds of the catch. Once in port the fish had to be raised out of the hold and sorted. Sailing trawlers all adopted auxiliary steam winches to haul in the heavy beam trawl. Most were built by Elliott & Garood of Beccles to their patent design of capstan with a steam engine mounted on top. The boiler chimney and the capstan can be seen in the centre of this picture.

Long-lining was an ancient method of deep-sea fishing. The lines were fitted with hundreds of baited hooks usually for catching cod. Aldeburgh maintained a small fleet of cod-bangers that sailed as far as Iceland in search of cod. The fish were kept alive in a specially constructed wet hold. The last one to sail was in 1914 and this picture shows two cod-bangers laid up at Aldeburgh with a smaller fishing smack and a group of yacht tenders and rowing boats for hire in the foreground.

Sailing trawlers remained competitive after the sailing drifters had given way to steam. Few steam trawlers were owned in Lowestoft before the 1920s. The first purpose-built steam trawler launched for Lowestoft owners was the *Loyalist* of 1914. Here a London-registered steam trawler is setting off the fishing grounds. For Lowestoft boats these were mainly in the North Sea rather than the more distant Iceland and Greenland waters.

The Lowestoft shipbuilders, Richards Ironworks, built the first locally owned diesel-engined trawler – the *Ala* – in 1931. New orders were scarce in the depressed years of the 1930s. After the Second World War the local trawling fleet was rebuilt and expanded. Many of them were built by the two local shipyards. The *Boston Arrow* (197 gross tons) was launched by Richards in 1959.

Sidewinder trawlers where the trawl net was worked over the side of the ship gave way to stern trawlers, like the *Suffolk Champion* (352 gross tons) of 1980, or pair-beam trawlers. One sidewinder, the *Mincarlo*, has been preserved at Lowestoft and is open to visitors in the summer. The *Suffolk Champion* only trawled for four years before conversion to an oil-rig stand by vessel. The last trawling company in the port – the Colne Fishing Co. – laid up its fleet in 2002 which probably means the end of deep-water trawling from Lowestoft.

# *Six*
# Leisure Craft

'Water frolics' or regattas, with sailing and rowing races which attracted much gambling and drinking, were popular holiday events in the early nineteenth century. Oulton Broad witnessed many such events including this one of 1827.

Oulton Broad became the centre of both yachting and cruising. Among the racing boats there is a white-hulled wherry yacht and in the background the Wherry Hotel, the social centre for yachtsmen.

Yachts were also raced on the North Sea at Lowestoft by the senior local yacht club, the Royal Norfolk & Suffolk Yacht Club. The club had a section of the harbour on the south side away from the bustle and smell of the fish markets to the north. However, their yachts, including the two large yawls and the steam yacht seen moored here, were probably manned in the summer season by fisherman for whom crewing yachts was valuable extra income.

Since the 1950s, fibre glass has taken over from wood as the main material for building yachts. Nevertheless, there are still some classic wooden boats to be seen such as the Broads cruiser on the left and the beautiful day sailing boat tied up to the modern fibre glass yacht, all laid up for the winter at St Olaves.

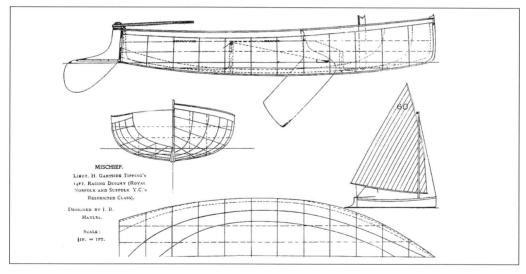

MISCHIEF.

LIEUT. H. GARTSIDE TIPPING'S 14FT. RACING DINGHY (ROYAL NORFOLK AND SUFFOLK Y.C.'S RESTRICTED CLASS).

DESIGNED BY I. R. HAYLES.

SCALE: ½IN. = 1FT.

Restricted class day sailing boats and dinghies became increasingly popular for racing in the early 1900s. It was a considerably cheaper pastime than owning of the large Victorian yachts which needed a paid crew. A sailing club would adopt a 'one design' and its fleet would be built to this particular specification. This made for much keener racing as much more depended on the talents of the crews. The 14ft racing dinghy adopted by the Royal Norfolk & Suffolk Yacht Club in 1911 is a good example of this new trend in racing.

Motor boats for cruising the Waveney and the Norfolk Broads became increasingly popular among individual owners and among the growing number of companies hiring out boats by the week. Small riverside villages such as St Olaves became centres for hire boats.

St Olaves was also home of Albatross speed boats. This Continentals Mark II had an aluminium hull fitted with an internal Ford 1,600cc engine and was built in 1959 for a Liverpool owner.

Today Fairline fast offshore cruisers are built at Ipswich Dock.

There has been a place for more sedate river and estuary day excursions. This Ipswich advertisement dates from the 1950s. It is interesting to note that it was managed from the Steam Boat Tavern, a reminder of the days when steam paddlers were the fastest means of travel to London from Ipswich.

Day cruises out to sea were popular. The Belle steamers' regular services from London have already been mentioned. Nicholson's, the tug owners of Great Yarmouth, ran the *Lord Nelson* and the *Lord Roberts* between Great Yarmouth and Lowestoft.

*Opposite, above:* Fritton Lake was an inland broad that was cut off from the Waveney but its beauty and improved access by rail made it a popular Victorian resort with rowing boats for hire.

*Opposite, below:* Leisure boating has boomed all along the Suffolk coast since the Second World War. The dock at Ipswich is virtually a marina with a small pocket of commercial activity. Recent years have also seen an influx of Dutch barges as house boats or sailing craft.

The *Ionia* was an old sailing trawler built at Grimsby in 1872 that had been beached at Aldeburgh as a holiday home. Her black tarry hull stood out among the marshes. Latterly she was allowed to fall into disrepair and she was deliberately burned in 1974. The Moot Hall at Aldeburgh displays this excellent model as a reminder of this distinctive holiday residence.

Boat trips have always been a component of seaside holidays. The opportunities for a trip round the bay or up the river have diminished since Victorian times. But one of the more interesting survivals in Suffolk is a trip along the winding channel of the Alde from Snape Maltings, which have been converted from an industrial complex into an arts centre.

Leisure boating has taken over in Suffolk's smaller ports. One hundred years ago, the dock at Woodbridge was a working berth for sailing barges and the famous tide mill was a working industrial plant receiving and shipping cargo and not a heritage landmark. At the same time, there were gentlemen's yachts based here and Robertson's, the oldest of Woodbridge's three yacht builders (the other two being Everson's and Whisstock's), was already busy with its own design of barge yachts.

Most modern yachts are rigged with a triangular Bermudan mainsail which does not have a gaff aloft to support the upper part of the sail. However, there has been a reaction against efficient mass-produced racing machines. Old wooden yachts have great appeal to growing minority of yachtsmen who want a classic boat. This fine example is off the Orwell and has all the romance and beauty of the great yachts tearing across Oulton Broad in 1900.

When maritime industries disappear, there is often a drive to preserve their memory among the local community they served. Lowestoft has a splendid maritime museum with a wonderful collection of paintings, models and relics of fishing craft, and is run by very knowledgeable volunteers.

Maritime museums can also be tourist attractions as well repositories of the local past. The International Sea Cadet Association's collection of boats was brought from Exeter to Oulton Broad. It contains a huge variety of boats anything from a Venetian gondola to boat made of reeds from Lake Titicaca. For various reasons the move has been unsuccessful and the collection is closed and in the process of moving to another location. Nevertheless Lowestoft is a centre for maritime preservation with the trawler's *Excelsior*, *City of Edinburgh* and *Mincarlo*, the drifter *Lydia Eva* and the Brooke Marine-built patrol vessel *Defender*.

# Seven
# Lifeboats and
# Service Vessels

The Suffolk Humane Society was founded in 1800 and raised funds for lifeboats along the coast, including one stationed at Orford. This engraving of 1838 depicts the wreck of the *Onion* close to the lighthouse at Orford Ness and the rescue boat may well be the Orford boat.

The shoals in the approaches to Lowestoft harbour are constantly moving and mariners are advised to take a pilot before entering the harbour.' That was the stark warning of the Admiralty Sailing Directions. The Lowestoft sailing trawler *Mercia* (presumably with an experienced local skipper) failed to avoid these shoals.

*Opposite, above:* Lightships that marked the offshore dangers of the East Coast were maintained by Trinity House at their Harwich depot. Lightships held in reserve were moored at Shotley on the Suffolk side of the Stour. Today, most lightships have either been automated or replaced by large automatic buoys and there was only one on standby in 2002.

*Opposite, below:* Surplus lightships have been sold off for preservation or for conversion to other uses, such as acting as a floating restaurant at Ipswich. Another retired lightship is based at the marina at Shotley.

It is probably not well known in Suffolk that Harvey's, the Ipswich shipbuilders, constructed two notable pilot schooners for the Liverpool Pilots: the *Leader* of 1856 and the *Perseverance* of 1860. This is the original half-model of the *Peseverance* which served at Liverpool until 1898. They also built another schooner for the River Elbe pilots in 1856.

The *Leader* worked on the Mersey approaches until 1896. Her most notable service was on 8 February 1886 when she led a large group of sailing vessels over the Mersey Bar to safety. The gale was too bad for pilots to board the vessels. The *Leader* and the *Persevrance* were a great testimony to the design talent and quality of building of the Ipswich shipbuilders.

Pilots with local expertise were essential for any visiting masters who were unfamiliar with the constantly shifting dangers at the entrances to the Blyth, Ore and Deben. The traffic to Aldeburgh justified a pilot cutter cruising off shore and this sailor-made model, on show in the Moot Hall, shows the Aldeburgh pilot boat was of similar design to the local long-lining cod smacks.

Dredging channels and docks became an essential service as ships grew in size. The first powered dredger in Suffolk was built by Jabez Bayley at Ipswich in 1828 for the Lowestoft & Norwich Navigation. The *W.D. Gateway* is one the largest and latest and works to deepen the approaches to the container berths at Felixstowe.

Cross-river ferries have also been an essential part of the Suffolk shipping scene since the Middle Ages. Most like that between Ferry Dock at Woodbridge and Sutton were no more than a ferryman in a rowing boat.

There were steam vehicle ferries that hauled themselves on chains laid across the River Deben between Felixstowe and Bawdsey, and the River Blyth between Southwold and Walberswick. The former lasted until the 1920s and the latter carried on until 1942.

There is an interesting ferry relic hanging in the yacht chandler's shop at Pin Mill: the old sign for Harry Ward's *Daisy Belle* which brought passengers ashore from the Great Eastern Railway's paddle steamers which made a scheduled stop at Pin Mill on their Ipswich to Harwich services.

The growth of the North Sea herring and trawling fisheries based on Lowestoft in the late nineteenth century brought with it the need for government supervision of fishery laws and protection against foreign interference. HMS *Hearty* was a powerful sea-going tug built in 1885 and was the first Fishery Protection vessel to be based at Lowestoft. She was armed with four three-pounder guns and had a top speed of 14 knots.

The torpedo gunboat HMS *Antelope* of 1893 was assigned fishery protection duties in the early 1900s. Although made obsolete in her first role by faster destroyers with steam turbines, she was impressive enough for fishery duties with two 4.7in and four three-pounder guns, plus torpedo tubes and a top speed of 19 knots. In the picture she is alongside the Fish Dock dressed overall, possibly on a regatta day.

The coastguard was set up in 1822 by HM Customs as an anti-smuggling service with shore stations along the Suffolk coast and cruisers offshore. In 1856 the service was transferred to the Admiralty. By the 1850s smuggling had declined and coastguards took on added responsibilities to assist with lifesaving and to act as a reserve for the Royal Navy. The *Squirrel* was one of its later cruisers seen here at Lowestoft. She was a 230-ton steamer with two three-pounder guns.

Coastguard lifesaving stations were also sited along the coast and were equipped with rocket firing equipment and breeches buoys to rescue the crews of ships that had come ashore.

Ship-repair facilities were an essential part of the Suffolk port's infrastructure. There might be no more than a 'grid iron' – a series of timbers on the shore for landing a ship on for repair work to be carried out at low tide. At Lowestoft, there was a public dry dock and several slipways owned by private firms. Colby's old repair yard has been taken by the Excelsior Trust and maintains its own fishing smack and other historic vessels such as the wherry *Albion*.

*Opposite, above:* Most ships are either lost at sea or broken up when they come to the end of their useful life. Ship breaking has been also been a minor local industry and continues at Ipswich. The *Prince Albert* was a former yacht which had been converted into a restaurant at Liverpool. It failed to meet the requirements of its licence and after years of lay up was towed to Ipswich for scrapping.

*Opposite, below:* HM Customs and Excise maintains patrols at sea. They are principally looking for drug smugglers and rather than regular patrols go to places where intelligence points to illegal activities. The *Vigilant* was at Ipswich for a crew change in December 2002.

Beach companies perform an essential service in the days of sail. Their fast seaworthy yawls could be used for the delivery of pilots, essential equipment and assistance such as manning pumps to ships in the offshore roadsteads. There are several companies between Lowestoft and Aldeburgh. The company at Kessingland had dressed their yawl overall for the local regatta.

The next three photographs were all taken at Lowestoft, possibly on the North Beach, and were part of a set showing a group of Rifle Volunteers enjoying their summer camp, c.1896-1899. This picture has several of them alongside one of the smaller single-masted gigs, with one of the larger two-masted yawls being readied for sea in the background.

The yawl is afloat while one crew man holds the bow and another stops her drifting sideways with an oar.

The yawl is hauled into deeper water using a rope warp which shackled to an anchor lying off the shore. This appears to be a pleasure trip with several soldiers on board. The mizzen sail is being raised.

Rowing and sailing lifeboats were stationed at different times all the way down the Suffolk coast from Corton to the Landguard Fort station at the entrance to the Orwell. In the nineteenth century there was no one standard lifeboat design. The Norfolk and Suffolk type evolved during the nineteenth century. It was essentially a beamy stable boat with built-in buoyancy but not self-righting. The *City of Winchester* of 1902 at 46ft (14m) long was the largest and served at Aldeburgh until 1928.

The *Mark Lane* (ex *Stock Exchange*) of 1890 was another Norfolk and Suffolk boat and was tested against other lifeboat designs by the RNLI on Lowestoft beach in February in 1892. She did not do well and had to be withdrawn. In later years she was converted into a house boat at Felixstowe Ferry. This fine model is part of the collection of Merseyside Maritime Museum, Liverpool.

RESCUE OF THE CREW OF THE STEAMER "SHAMROCK," OF DUBLIN, BY THE LOWESTOFT LIFE-BOA T.

A great gale in October 1859 saw the paddle steamer *Dublin* run aground on the Holm Sands off Lowestoft. The Lowestoft lifeboat succeeded in rescuing all the crew of fourteen by dragging them through the water on lines. The lifeboat skipper and six of the crew were awarded silver medals by the RNLI for their feat.

Pakefield had two lifeboat stations; the first was established in 1840 and closed in 1922, and the second served between 1871 and 1895. The five lifeboats stationed here saved 273 lives.

Southwold lifeboat station was by a local lifeboat society in 1841, which was later taken over by the RNLI with a second station established in 1866. The second lasted until 1920 and the first until 1940. Their lifeboats saved 190 lives. Today, there is in an inshore rescue boat stationed here.

This engraving depicts Southwold Society's boat *Harriet* battling out to save the crew of a ship ashore on the outer shoals on 22 February 1862.

Lifeboats have always been run with voluntary donations and volunteer crews. 'Lifeboat Days' were popular summer events. The Southwold lifeboat *Alfred Corry* was being admired by a huge crowd before a demonstration launch in 1908.

A second picture of the same demonstration shows the launching carriage and the crew aboard ready to haul her out through the surf.

The crew of the *Alfred Corry* used the hauling-out warp to get her into deeper water and have set the mizzen lug sail.

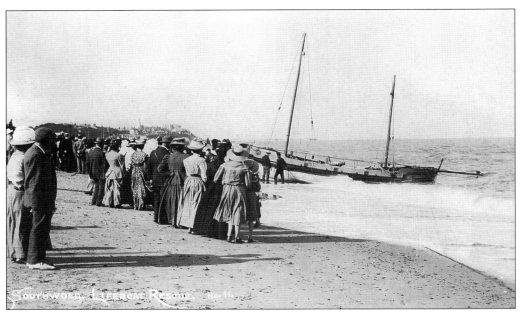

The return to the beach could be more hazardous than the launch and even in the fine weather of a summer's day the risk from the surf capsizing the boat is clear.

The Aldeburgh lifeboat *Aldeburgh* of 1890 had an outstanding record of service when she was launched for the last time on 7 December 1899. She appeared to have got clear of the surf when a huge wave capsized her and drove her back on the beach. Seven of the crew were trapped inside the boat, and frantic efforts were made to get them out.

The *Aldeburgh* lying on the beach after the disaster. A hole had been cut in the side of the hull and a heavy spar used in attempt to lever her up.

LIFE BOAT AND BEACH, ALDEBURGH

*Above:* The *Aldeburgh* was replaced by the *City of Winchester* in 1902 and this picture shows her on station on Aldeburgh beach. Recently the modern Aldeburgh boat has been housed in its own lifeboat house of a strikingly modern design.

*Left:* The *City of Winchester* returning to Aldeburgh under sail.

James Cable was the finest of the Aldeburgh lifeboat coxswains. He was born in 1851 and went into deep-sea sailing ships. On his return to Aldeburgh he joined the lifeboat crew and did not retire until 1917. He was ill with flu on the day of the *Aldeburgh* disaster and was forbidden by the doctor to take the boat out. He supervised the rescue efforts. He won the RNLI's medal and added two bars to it as well as medals from the Royal Humane Society and from Norway and Sweden.

The lifeboat heritage of the county is not only contained in photographs but in models and paintings. This 'primitive' painting depicts the lifeboat station at Dunwich, *c*.1880.

Another piece of this heritage is housed in the former lifeboat house that used to be at the end of Cromer pier. This is sailing and rowing lifeboat *Alfred Corry*, the Southwold lifeboat between 1893 and 1918, is being restored and is open to the public at Southwold harbour.